AF372087

WESTERN STEAM
in camera

John Adams and
Patrick Whitehouse

LONDON
IAN ALLAN LTD

First published 1976

ISBN 0 7110 0695 4

Published by Ian Allan Ltd, Shepperton, Surrey,
and printed in the United Kingdom by
Ian Allan Printing Ltd.

Above:
"Dukedog" 4-4-0 No 9017 assists 4-6-0 No 7818
Granville Manor out of Shrewsbury on the down "Cambrian
Coast Express" on 2nd September 1960.   Photo: G. England.

WESTERN STEAM IN CAMERA

There is nothing new in an album of railway pictures — indeed one could almost say that a plethora of them exists already. Nevertheless trains never cease to attract and steam trains of yesteryear provide nostalgia for the mature and excitement for those who did not know them as an everyday event — witness the 350,000 people who turned up to watch the 150th anniversary parade of engines at Shildon. In this series of ''Steam in Camera'' we look at locomotives and trains from Nationalisation in 1948 to the end of regular steam in Britain, beginning with the Western and what remained of ''God's Wonderful Railway''. The Great Western somehow had the mystique which appealed to those who loved that sense of order comfort and efficiency, and their green engines with flashing brass and copper chimney caps lasted until 1965. Even today it is Great Western engines which haul the only steam trains on British Rail tracks; though sadly painted blue their Swindon characteristics are plain enough. This small collection of pictures gives a cross-section of Western trains at work over the period and it is hoped that it will give pleasure to those who loved any steam locomotives, let alone ''Castles'' and ''Kings''. Where possible dates have been given in detail in the captions to enable the pictures to have an historic interest in addition to a visual one.

''Castle'' 4-6-0 No 5067 *St Fagans Castle* at approximately 70mph on the 1·15pm Paddington to Bristol express near Thingley Junction in June, 1951.
Photo: P. M. Alexander.

1948 to 1952
STEAM IS STILL SUPREME

The first five years of nationalisation brought little change to the Great Western Railway — for sure "Kings" were painted blue for a while and chocolate-and-cream coaches appeared in colours reminiscent of those of the County Donegal Railways Joint Committee in Ireland, but that was about all there was to it. Stationmasters still kept their badge of office in a type of GWR fez, signalmen their waistcoats and polished levers and double-framed "Dukedogs" plied to and fro over ex Cambrian metals. True, a few "Britannia" Pacifics were sent to work South Wales trains, but they bore good old Great Western names like *Shooting Star* and *Mercury*. New "Castles" were being built as late as 1950. All was well in the Land of Grand.

"Star 4-6-0 No 4039 *Queen Matilda* being prepared at Hereford Loco Depot on 6th November 1948 for a Cardiff train. It is in almost original condition without outside steam pipes.
P. M. Alexander.

Just GWR: One of Collett's 'Duke/Bulldog' rebuilds,
No 9028, between Machynlleth and Dovey
Junction on the Cambrian section of the GWR in
1947.
Photo: P. M. Alexander.

38XX 2-8-0 No 2893 on a down goods, assisted in
the rear, climbs Dainton Bank near Stoneycombe,
on 3rd March, 1950.
Photo: P. M. Alexander.

2-6-2T No 4179 in ''LNW'' livery, piloting 4-6-0
No 5029 *Nunney Castle* on the down morning
newspaper train near Stoneycombe on 25th March
1950.
Photo: P. M. Alexander.

2-8-2T No 7220 on a down goods assisted in the rear by 4-6-0 No 6934 *Beachamwell Hall* passing Stoneycombe Quarry Siding on 25th March 1950. Photo: P. M. Alexander.

One of the few remaining "Saints", No 2915 *Saint Bartholomew* takes a down express past Bentley Heath crossing near Knowle and Dorridge on 14th May 1949.
Photo: C. F. H. Oldham.

A latter-day "Star" in the evening of her days.
No 4051 *Princess Helena* takes a Birmingham Snow Hill to Worcester semi-fast out of Stratford-upon-Avon on 10th April, 1950.
Photo: C. F. H. Oldham.

The 11·27am Leamington Spa to Worcester via Stratford-upon-Avon nears the summit of Hatton Bank in April 1950. The engine is GWR No 3377 (originally named *Penzance*) — a "Bulldog" of 1903.
Photo: P. M. Alexander.

"County" class 2-cylinder 4-6-0 No 1020 *County of Monmouth* in black livery lined out in red, off-white and yellow, at Swindon on 10th September 1950.
Photo: P. M. Alexander.

As built with a single chimney No 1013 *County of Dorset* carrying her new 83F shed code, near St Erth on 16th June 1950.
Photo: C. F. H. Oldham

Complete with train of Hawksworth stock,
No 5021 moves out of St Erth on 16th June 1950.
Photo: C. F. H. Oldham

2-6-2T No 5570 heads the down "Cambrian Coast
Express" near Criccieth on 18th September 1950.
Photo: C. F. H. Oldham.

"Saint" class 4-6-0 No 2943 *Hampton Court*
approaching Twerton Tunnel near Bath, with a
Bristol to Swindon stopping train, in brilliant
sunshine after a thunder shower on 11th
September 1950.
Photo: P. M. Alexander.

"Castle" class 4-6-0 No 5056 *Earl of Powis*
glittering in new green paint and polished copper
and brass at Swindon Works on 8th October 1950.
Photo: P. M. Alexander

OVERLEAF

The "Merchant Venturer", a Paddington-Bristol
express of the 1950s. The 13-coach train is hauled
by an unidentified but hard-working Castle.
Photo: P. M. Alexander.

Dean Goods 0-6-0 No 2349 runs in to Creedenhill
station in September 1950 with a Hereford to
Brecon (via Three Cocks Junc.) branch train.
Photo: P. B. Whitehouse.

TELEPHONE
CREDENHILL
2349

THE MERCHANT VENTURER

"Star" class 4-6-0 No 4055 *Princess Sophia* on
the 4·07 pm Swindon to Bristol mixed passenger
and milk train leaving Twerton tunnel.
Photo: P. M. Alexander.

No 6023 *King Edward II* in immaculate blue livery
skirting the shores of the Exe estuary on the down
"Cornish Riviera Express" near Starcross on 20th
February 1951.
Photo: P. M. Alexander.

Ex-LNER Class V2 2-6-2 No 60845 on test from
Swindon Works heads the GWR dynamometer car
with a test train near Hullavington during the
winter of 1950.
Photo: P. M. Alexander.

2-6-2T No 4109 on the 10·45am Newton Abbot to Exeter St Davids train (stopping at all stations) leaves Teignmouth and approaches the sea wall on 23rd February 1951.
Photo: P. M. Alexander.

"Dean Goods" 0-6-0 No 2460 hauling "Grange" 4-6-0 No 6840 *Hazeley Grange* to Swindon Works for overhaul and repair, near Chalford-Frampton Crossing on 22nd March 1951. The "Grange" has her rods removed and the "Dean" is making heavy weather of the 1 in 58 gradient up to Sapperton Tunnel.
Photo: P. M. Alexander.

''Dean Goods'' 0-6-0 No 2541 shunting on the daily pick-up freight from Hereford to Brecon at Kinnersley, Herefordshire on 24th March 1951.
Photo: P. M. Alexander.

"Hall" 4-6-0 No 6939 *Calveley Hall* drawing into Birmingham Snow Hill with the coaches for the afternoon train to Cardiff, on 15th August 1951.
Photo: P. M. Alexander.

Ex Cambrian Railways 0-6-0 No 89 as GWR No 887 (built 1903 by R. Stephenson) heads the daily freight from Brecon to Oswestry on 17th August 1951.
Photo: P. M. Alexander.

''Dukedog'' 4-4-0 No 9027 on the 12·00 mid-day
Aberystwyth all stations to Oswestry and Salop, at
Moat Lane Junction on 17th August 1951.
Photo: P. M. Alexander.

A Cambrian 0-6-0 as GWR No 887 with the Brecon Line train (2·40 pm to all stations, including Llanidloes, Rhyader and Builth Wells) at Moat Lane Junction on 17th August 1951.
Photo: P. M. Alexander.

''Manor'' class 4-6-0 No 7813 *Freshford Manor* piloting ''County'' 4-6-0 No 1018 *County of Leicester* on the 12·28pm Plymouth North Road to Newton Abbot, stopping at all sttions, climbing the 1 in 42 gradient up Hemerdon Bank on 9th October 1951.
Photo: P. M. Alexander.

OVERLEAF
King George VI's funeral: The guests' special train near Slough on 15th February 1952 behind No 7004 *Eastnor Castle*.
Photo: M. W. Earley.

BR Class 7 4-6-2 No 70022 *Tornado*
departing from Bristol Temple Meads on
22nd November 1951 with the 9·25am
Manchester London Road to Plymouth.
Bath Road Loco Depot on right.
Photo: P. M. Alexander.

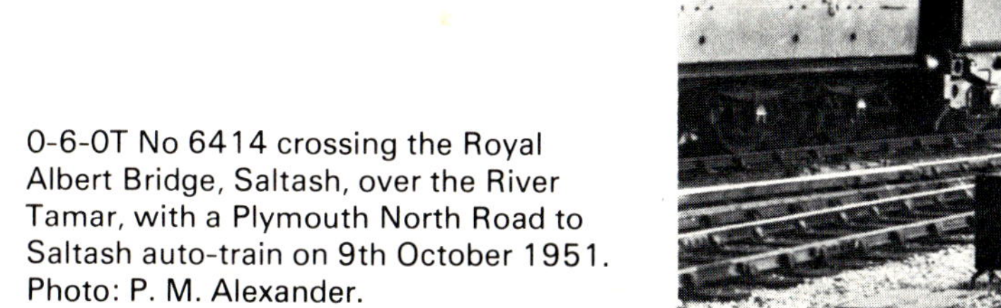

0-6-0T No 6414 crossing the Royal
Albert Bridge, Saltash, over the River
Tamar, with a Plymouth North Road to
Saltash auto-train on 9th October 1951.
Photo: P. M. Alexander.

Star class No 4059 *Princess Patricia* with a down
express near Minety on 19th April 1952.
Photo: P. M. Alexander.

47XX Class 2-8-0 No 4702 in LNWR livery. The
engine is running in after an overhaul at Swindon
Works and is heading the 11·23am Bath to
Swindon stopping train near Langley Crossing
Chippenham on 23rd June, 1952.
Photo: P. M. Alexander.

0-6-0PT No 8783 on the evening freight from
Calne to Chippenham, leaving Calne on 16th July
1952.
Photo: P. M. Alexander.

0-4-2T No 1433 sets out into the snow-clad countryside with the 11·53am Chippenham to Calne on 1st December 1952.
Photo: P. M. Alexander.

"Hall" class 4-6-0 No 4912 *Berrington Hall* near the summit of Dauntsey Bank on 30th November 1952 with the 9·35am (Sundays) Weymouth to Swindon. Photo: P. M. Alexander.

38XX class 2-8-0 No 3829 takes a Salop
to South Wales freight over the summit at
Llanvihangel in 1953.
Photo: P. M. Alexander.

Ex-ROD 2-8-0 GWR No 3036 grinding up
the long 1 in 300 bank between
Brinkworth and Badminton with a freight
to South Wales on 4th February 1953.
Photo: P. M. Alexander.

1953 to 1957
THE WIND OF CHANGE
BEGINS TO BLOW

As the 1950s rolled on steam still ruled, but the older engines began to go to their last rest and inroads started into suburban and some branch lines by the diesel multiple-units. This period saw the full demise of the "Saints" and "Stars", the Cambrian 0-6-0s and the double-framed Dean and Churchward engines. Standard locomotoves began to appear on the lines from Three Cocks Junction and on the Cambrian section and rolling stock began to be painted in LMS red. But there was an Indian Summer. In 1957 Reggie Hanks, an ex-Swindon apprentice, became Chairman of the Western Region Board, whilst a Government innovation gave more authority to the Regions. Coaches once again appeared in chocolate and cream on the more important trains, green became the universal livery for all locomotives; no longer did "Halls" and "Manors" appear in pseudo LNWR livery, and *City of Truro* came out of York Museum to work WR specials. But it was not to last.

BR Class 7 4-6-2 No 70029 *Shooting Star*, near the summit of the 1 in 300 bank through Sodbury, on the up "Red Dragon" on 6th February 1953. Milepost 100 from Paddington is at this point. Photo: P. M. Alexander.

The down ''Merchant Venturer'', Paddington-
Bristol, passing Thingley West Junction behind
4-6-0 No 5055 *Earl of Eldon* in March 1953.
Photo: P. M. Alexander.

''Castle'' 4-6-0 No 5021 *Whittington Castle*
breasting the summit of the 1 in 100 out of Box
Tunnel with the 12·00 noon Bristol to Paddington
on 27th March 1953.
Photo: P. M. Alexander.

55XX 2-6-2T No 5553 on a Bristol to Chippenham
train near Thingley on 11th May 1953.
Photo: P. M. Alexander.

For many years the Churchward Moguls ran the Ruabon to Barmouth trains via Dolgelly. Here is No 6367 shortly after leaving Penmaenpool on a May Saturday in 1954.
Photo: P. B. Whitehouse.

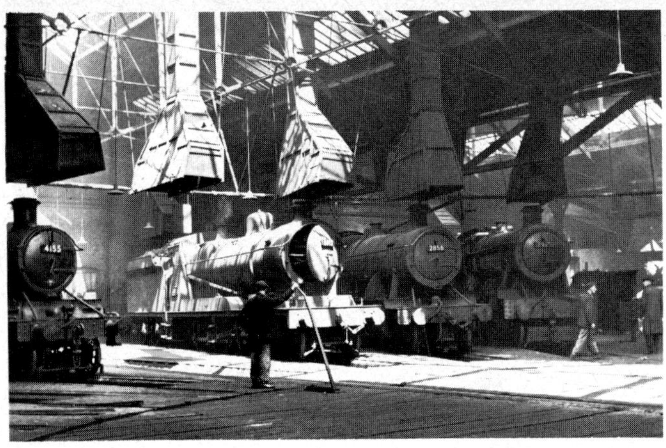

Family Group: Ex-GWR engines inside the roundhouse at Tyseley Shed, Birmingham in the summer of 1953.
Photo: P. B. Whitehouse.

GWR 0-4-2T No 1403 heads a Chippenham to Calne Branch train near Hazeland, circa 1953.
Photo: P. M. Alexander.

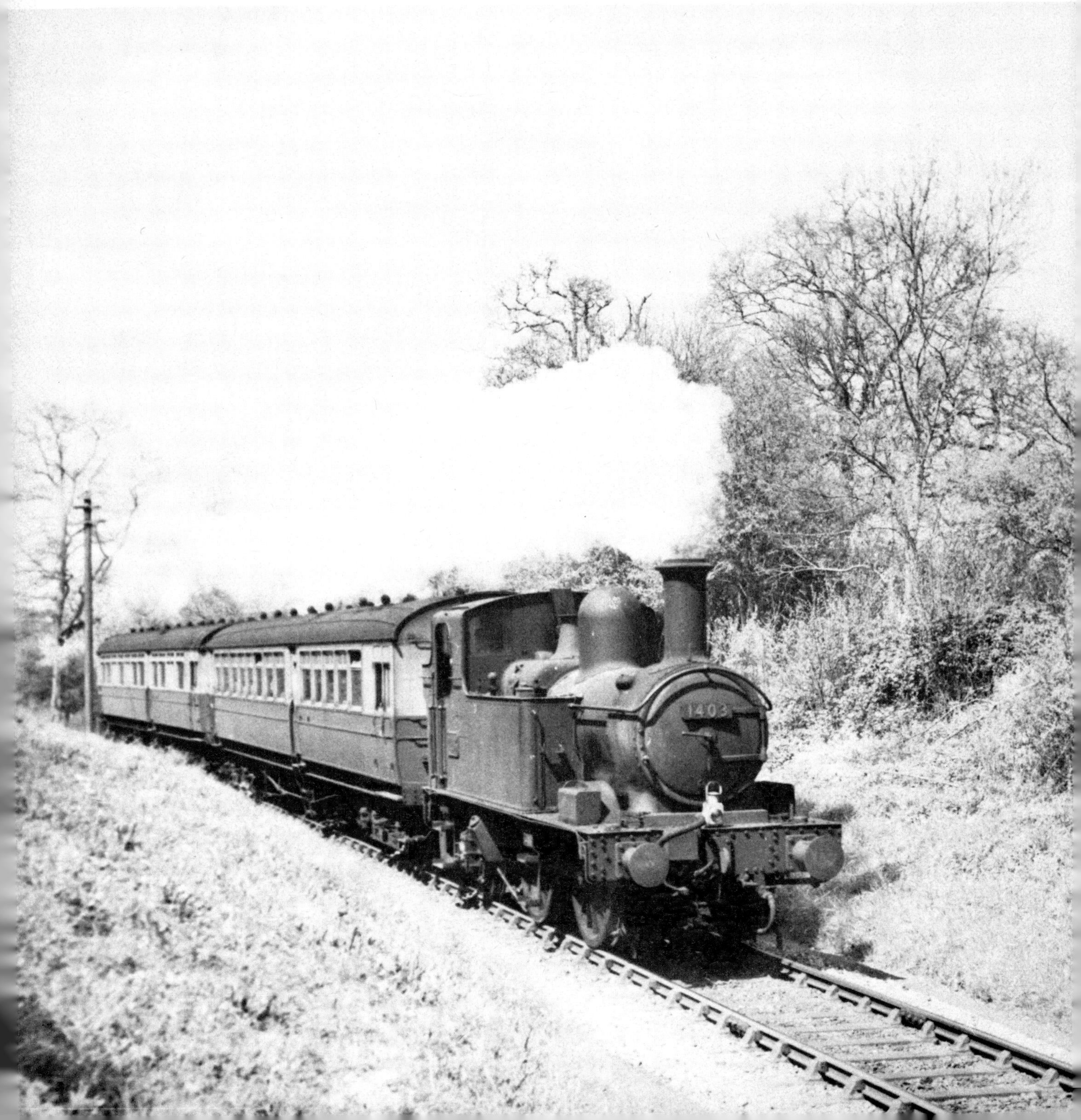

6134

A Festiniog Railway Society Special from London to Minfford shortly after crossing Barmouth viaduct. The train has been double-headed by two ''Dukedogs'' from Shrewsbury.
Photo: P. B. Whitehouse.

Visitor from the South: displaced from London area, suburban service, 2-6-2T No 6134 spends a short while at Tyseley Shed on similar duties.
Photo: P. B. Whitehouse.

OVERLEAF
A Liverpool-Plymouth express climbing Dainton Bank behind ''Manor'' class 4-6-0 No 7813 *Freshford Manor* (fitted with intermediate-size tender) piloting ''Hall'' class 4-6-0 No 7916 *Mobberley Hall* on 22nd September 1954.
Photo: David S. Fish.

7813

''Dukedog'' 4-4-0 No 9020 near Picnic Island,
Aberdovey in June 1955.
Photo: P. B. Whitehouse.

Heavy work on Dainton: a westbound train headed
by BR standard Class 4 No 75026 and an unknown
''Castle'' nearing the summit of Dainton Bank on
18th June 1955.
Photo: P. B. Whitehouse.

OPPOSITE
During the 1950s the London Midland Region took over the operation of the old Cambrian section and replaced the ex-Great Western engines with BR Standards. Here is the up "Cambrian Coast Express" climbing Talerddig bank behind Standard class 4 4-6-0 No 75005 in April 1956.
Photo: P. B. Whitehouse.

City of Truro came out of retirement in York museum during 1957 to be used, in the main, for enthusiast specials. This train is the annual Stephenson Locomotive Society special to Swindon works returning home to Birmingham, climbing Hatton Bank on the evening of 16th June 1957.
Photo: R. J. Blenkinsop.

OVERLEAF
The up "Torbay Express" leaving Kingswear behind Castle class No 5053 *Earl Cairns* on 18th September 1957. The loco in foreground is No 7029 *Clun Castle*.
Photo: David S. Fish.

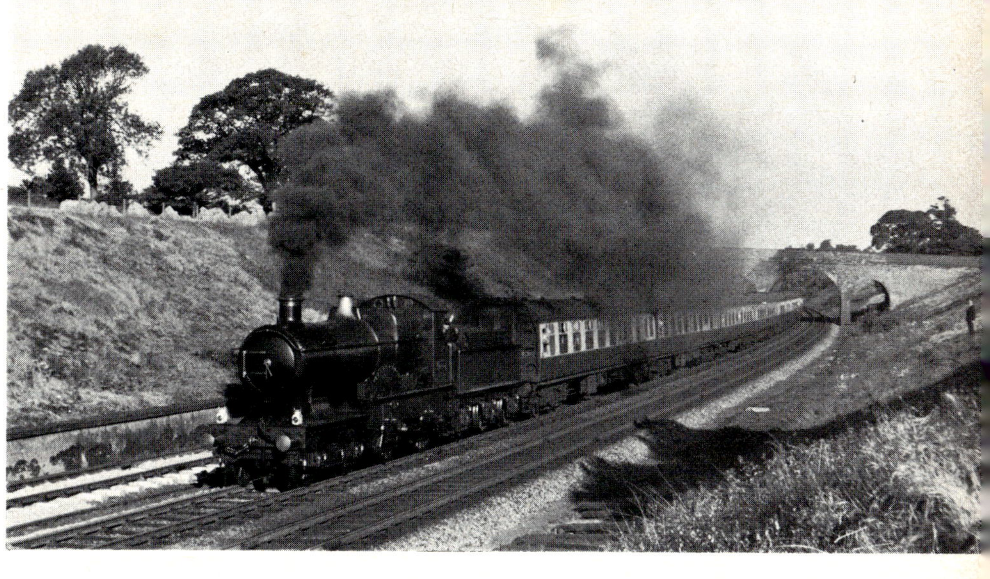

4-6-0 No 7914 *Lleweni Hall* pilots a "King" 4-6-0 past Dainton signalbox with a St Ives-Paddington express in August 1957.
Photo: G. D. King.

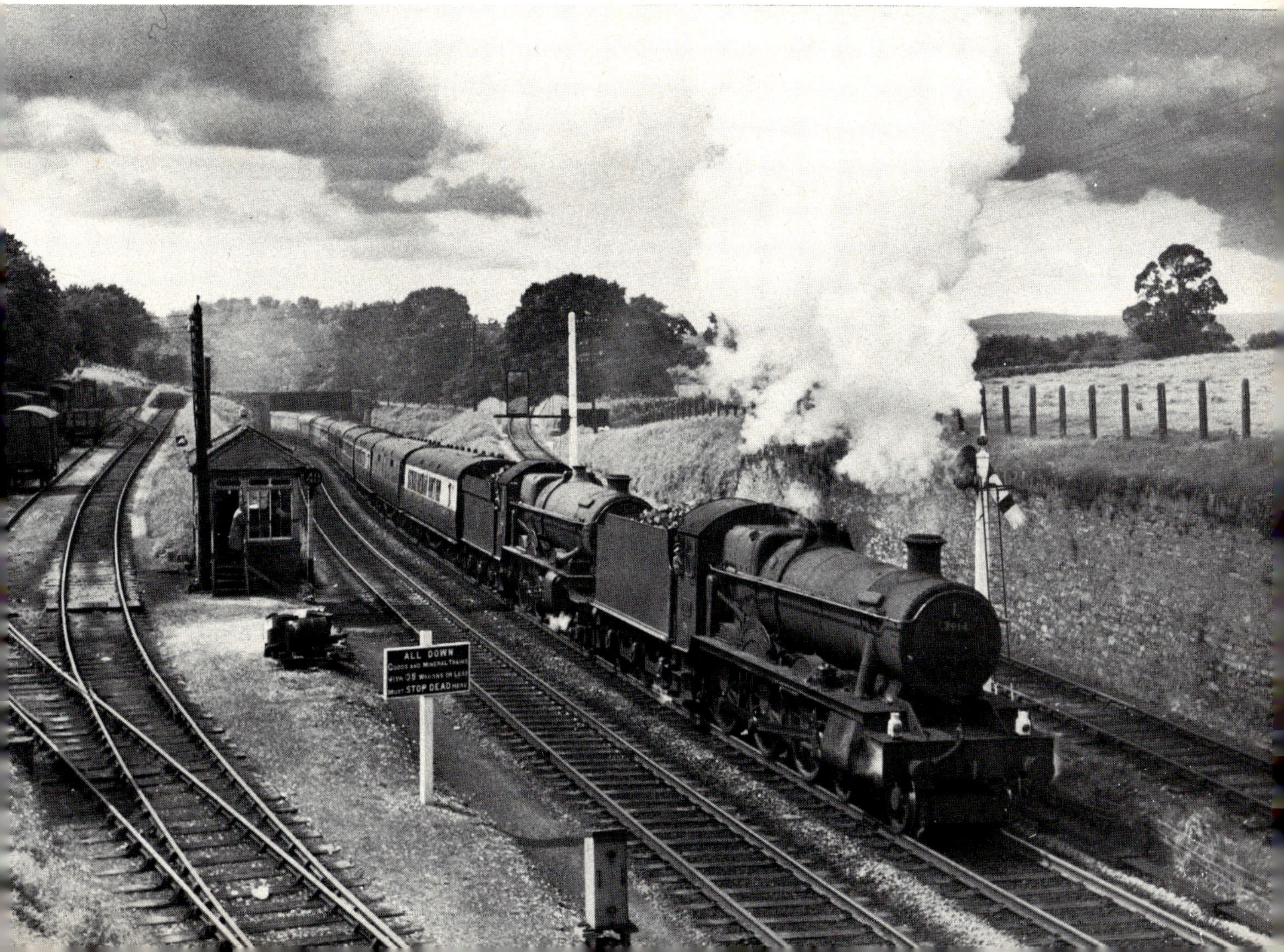

1958 to 1965
THE FINAL YEARS

By 1960 Stanley Raymond had been sent to Paddington as General Manager, and the break-up of the Great Western began in earnest. Regional boundaries were redrawn, giving the London Midland the Cambrian coast sections but the Western the Lickey incline. Diesels (the Western alone had diesel-hydraulics) took over the expresses from "Kings" and "Castles" and sheds began to close. The last route for main-line GWR steam was Worcester to Paddington. The coming of Gerry Fiennes to the chair of the Western in 1964 brought back something of the spirit of the old days, but by the close of 1965 GWR steam, bar that thoughtfully preserved, had gone, LMS engines haunted Banbury, Tyseley, Oxley and Birkenhead; and only Nos 7, 8 and 9 remained hard at work during the summer on the Rheidol line. Today Great Western steam still runs from Aberystwyth and from privately-owned depots like Didcot and Tyseley; it is also at home on the Dart Valley lines out of Totnes and Paignton. But the old days are gone.

The 10am Birmingham Snow Hill-Paddington accelerates away from Leamington Spa behind No 6005 *King George I* in October, 1958.
Photo: R. J. Blenkinsop.

Between the tunnels, Dawlish. July 1958.
Photo: Eric Oldham.

CAPITALS
UNITED
EXPRESS
063

BR standard class 7 Pacific No 70020
Mercury storms out of Patchway tunnel
with the up "Capitals United Express" in
May 1959.
Photo: G. F. Heiron.

Grand Finale: On 18th March 1960 the
very last steam locomotive to be built for
British Railways, Class 9 2-10-0
No 92220, was named *Evening Star* at
Swindon Works. With *North Star* and
"Western" diesels in the background, the
crowd listens to Keith Grand and Reggie
Hanks.
Photo: British Railways.

Pride of the Western: the eastbound "Bristolian"
roars along the embankment at Westerleigh in
November, 1959.
Photo: George F. Heiron.

A Crewe-built class 2 2-6-0 takes a Dolgelly train
out of Barmouth in September 1962.
Photo: P. B. Whitehouse.

55XX class 2-6-2T No 5541 crosses Riverford
Viaduct on the long climb through the vale of
Bickleigh with the 3·05pm Plymouth-Launceston
train on 10th May 1961.
Photo: Peter F. Bowles.

"County" class 4-6-0 No 1011 *County of Chester*
with a Taunton to London train (via Bristol) passing
through Bath on 11th August 1961.
Photo: Derek Cross.

The last "Star": No 4056 *Princess Margaret* with her old GWR number painted on the buffer beam, awaits a Stephenson Locomotive Society special train to Swindon at Tyseley shed Birmingham in June 1955.
Photo: P. B. Whitehouse.

Saturdays-only morning trip to Culmstock, with 0-4-2T No 1450 running round its one coach, on 22nd June, 1963.
Photo: G. D. King.

2-6-0 No 7333 at Venn Cross with a Barnstaple-Taunton train of SR stock in August 1961. Note the design of the signal, allowing it to be sighted through Venn Cross tunnel.
Photo: M. J. Fox.

OVERLEAF

Saved from the breaker's torch, GWR 2-6-2T No 4555, restored to GWR livery, follows 4-6-0 No 7827 *Lydham Manor* out of Towyn station on a Talyllyn Railway Preservation Society special in September 1964. Both locomotives are now at work on the Dart Valley Light Railway in South Devon.
Photo: M. Pope.

7827

On 4th May 1964 the Western Region, in conjunction with Ian Allan Ltd, ran the last high-speed steam train from Paddington to Plymouth and return with the expressed aim of attaining 100mph between Bristol and London. The engine chosen for this section was No 5054 *Earl of Ducie*. Though the attempt failed to reach the maximum this special was duly filmed by the BBC for their new Second Channel Programmes and prior to the trip *Earle of Ducie* made a series of special photo runs. She is seen here at Honeybourne on Wednesday 1st May.
Photo: P. B. Whitehouse.

For the BR/Ian Allan special on 4th May 1964 reserve ''Castles'' were stationed at strategic points in case of failure: in the event No 7025 *Sudeley Castle* had to take over from No 4079 *Pendennis Castle* on the outward journey. No 7032 *Denbigh Castle*, one of the 1950-built ''Castles'' was kept at Bristol for possible use on the last lap of the return trip, but not used. It is interesting to ponder on the possible use of No 7032 with its double chimney — maybe she *might* have made the elusive 100mph.
Photo: P. B. Whitehouse.

Restored GW 2-6-2T No 4555 working a Birmingham–Leamington pick-up freight near
Hatton during the summer of 1964.
Photo: Tom Williams.

During Mr Fiennes' reign at Paddington
the two ''Castles'' now in preservation
were saved with his active co-operation.
Here is the first to be withdrawn,
No 4079 *Pendennis Castle,* near Beam
Bridge on the climb to Whiteball tunnel on
2nd October 1965.
Photo: G. D. King.

Single-line working: The double-headed "Cambrian Coast Express" thunders up to Talerddig Summit and passes a Machynlleth-bound train waiting for the road during September 1964.
Photo: P. B. Whitehouse.

With the handing over of the Cambrian Coast line to the London Midland Region BR standard locomotives came to be shedded at Machynlleth. This unidentified class 4MT stands outside the shed in September 1966.
Photo: P. B. Whitehouse.

Now that steam has vanished from the main lines
of British Railways Great Western engines can still
be found at work on the Dart Valley Light Railway
in Devon as well as from steam centres such as
Didcot and Tyseley. 0-6-0PT No 1369 stands in
steam at Buckfastleigh in readiness for a special to
Ashburton for carnival celebrations on 12th July
1967.
Photo: John M. Boyes.

British Railways' only steam-operated line, the 2ft 0in-gauge Vale of Rheidol. No 8 *Owain Glyndwr* takes the morning train up beyond Aberffrwd on a dull morning in June 1970.
Photo: Colourviews Picture Library.